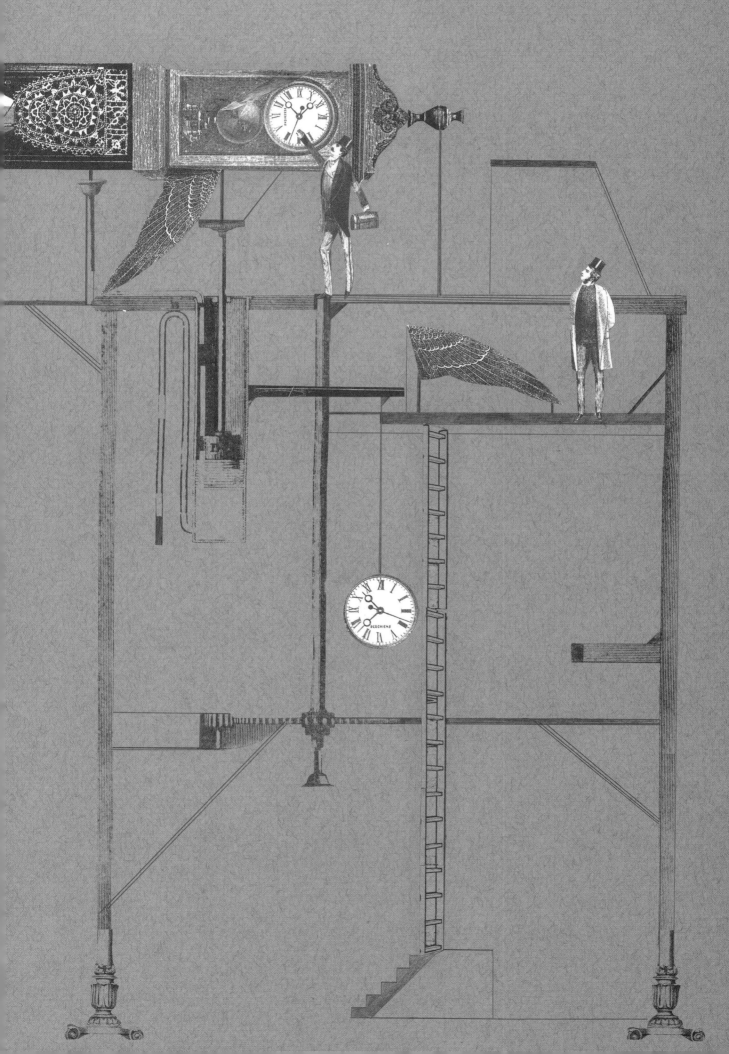

For Nic and Hac
– always on time
M. J.

For Grandad
love
Richard

Text copyright © 2009 by Martin Jenkins
Illustrations copyright © 2009
by Richard Holland

First U.S. edition 2009

Library of Congress
Cataloging-in-Publication Data

Jenkins, Martin, date. The time book: a brief history from lunar calendars to atomic clocks/Martin Jenkins; illustrated by Richard Holland.—1st U.S. ed.
p. cm.

ISBN 978-0-7636-4112-2
1. Time—Juvenile literature. 2. Time measurements—Juvenile literature.
3. Calendar—Juvenile literature. I. Holland, Richard, 1976- ill. II. Title.
QB209.5.J455 2009
529'.7—dc22
2008019706

2 4 6 8 10 9 7 5 3 1

Printed in China

This book was typeset in Amasis MT.
The illustrations were done in mixed media.

Candlewick Press
99 Dover Street
Somerville, Massachusetts 02144

visit us at www.candlewick.com

CANDLEWICK PRESS

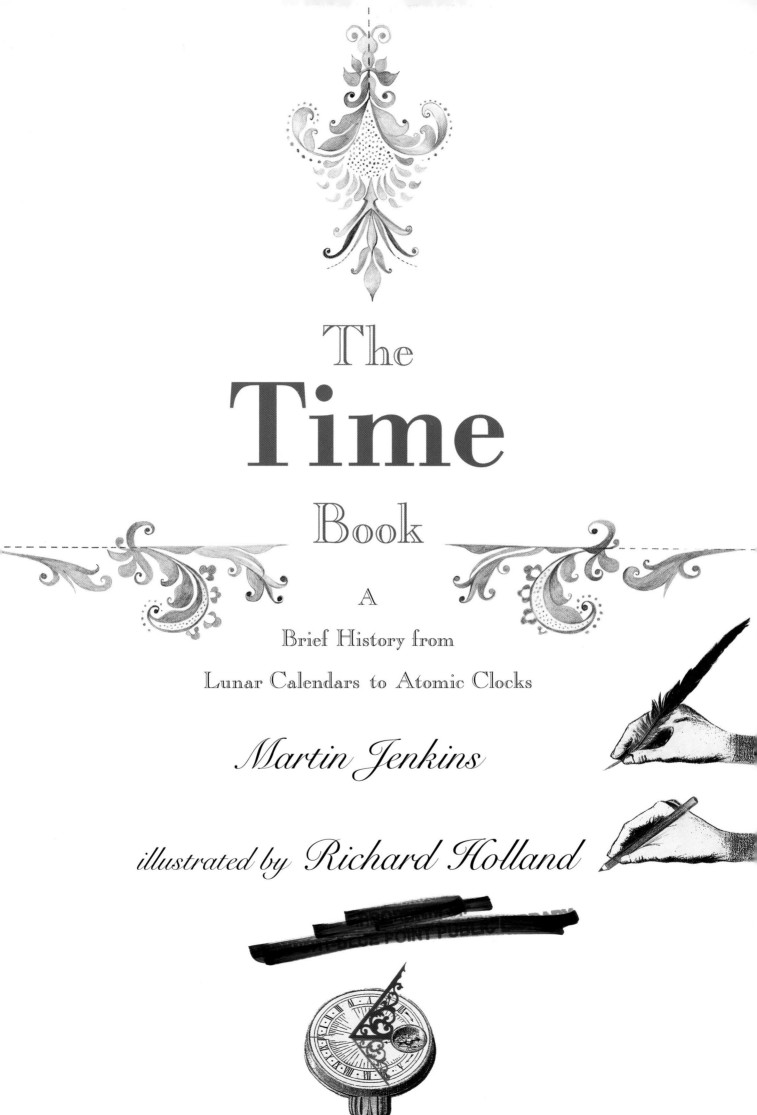

The Time Book

A

Brief History from

Lunar Calendars to Atomic Clocks

Martin Jenkins

illustrated by *Richard Holland*

i'm having fun

Chapter One

Everybody knows that time flies when you're having fun, and I'm sure we'd all agree that it drags when you're not.

But even if it feels that way, surely all time is the same, and any minute is the same as any other minute—exactly 60 seconds long? And aren't minutes just a handy way of chopping up longer periods of time into nice, regular, bite-size chunks? We all know there are 60 of them in an hour, 24 hours in a day, and seven days in a week. And if we do the math, that equals 10,080 minutes or 168 hours in a week. But that's a bit strange, isn't it? Why 10,080 minutes and not 10,000? Why aren't time units measured in neat, round numbers?

Clock Riding
5 hour wait

i'm not having fun

We humans generally like our measurements to stay the same—a foot is always 12 inches, never 11 or 13. But time units aren't all like that. Take months. Some have 30 days, some 31, and one, poor old February, has only 28—that is, except for every four years, when it has 29. Well, not quite every four years, because in most years that end in 00 (like 1800 and 1900), it has only 28 again, even though (according to the four-year rule) it should have 29. And then every 400 years, it has 29 again (like in the year 2000). All of which means that years have 365 days, except when they have 366, which is every four years, except when it isn't. Confused? I'm not surprised.

So why are our ways of measuring time so bizarre? Why are months and years not all the same length, and why don't weeks divide neatly into

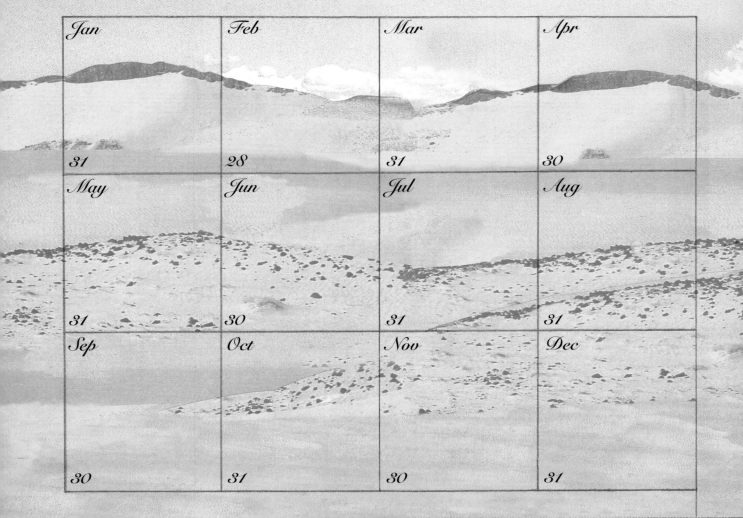

months and years? And come to think of it, why are there 60 minutes in an hour, not 40 or 80 or ten, and why are there seven days in a week and 365 (or so) days in a year?

And why are we so obsessed with counting and measuring and keeping time, anyway? Why does it seem so important to know the exact time and date all the time? Was it always like this? Did people always get angry if you were two minutes late for class or for the dentist? Two thousand years ago, would you have missed your trireme or your camel train if you turned up at 11:01 instead of 10:59? If we didn't always live our lives by the clock, when did we start, and why?

And while we're at it, what is this stuff called time, anyway?

Chapter Two

Humans are the only animals that have invented calendars and mechanical clocks, but it seems that most, perhaps all, other living things have ways of measuring time. We know this because virtually all of them do certain things at certain times quite regularly. A lot of plants flower at a particular time of year, regardless of the weather, and many kinds of birds fly off in the autumn to warmer regions, leaving the places where they breed at almost exactly the same time year after year.

It might be that they're just reacting to changes going on around them—it gets cooler in the fall, and the days get shorter. And it's true that changes like these do often affect plants and animals. For example, you can fool a lot of plants into flowering at the wrong time of year by changing the temperature and giving them lots of extra light. But it's not that simple. Experimenters have kept migrating birds cut off from the outside world for years in rooms where the temperature never changes

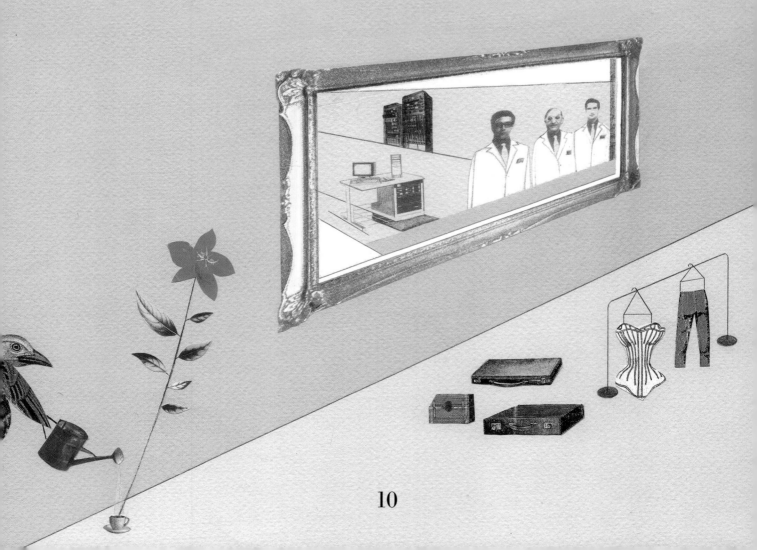

and with the same number of hours of light and dark each day, and the birds still try to migrate in the fall. And squirrels kept this way start to grow fat and sleepy in preparation for hibernation at around the same time that they would in the wild. Somehow they keep track of the time throughout the year.

Some animals do even better than that. In North America, there's an insect called a periodical cicada that lives for years and years as a larva underground, feeding on tree roots, before emerging one summer to breed. Some broods stay underground for 13 years and some for 17 years. Somehow the broods always get the number of years exactly right—they never pop up after 12 or 14 or 18 years. We know that changes in the chemicals in the tree roots during spring tell the larvae that a new year has arrived, but we still don't understand how the insects know when the right number of years has passed.

Timekeeping takes place on a much shorter scale, too. Honeybees seem to be able to time their flights. They can also work out how fast they are flying (by measuring the speed at which objects whiz past their eyes). They can combine these two things to work out how far from their hive a particular patch of flowers is. What's more, they can tell all this to their hivemates. When a scout bee finds a particularly good patch of flowers, she collects some pollen or nectar and zips back to her hive. Other bees cluster around while the bee performs a dance. If the flowers are nearby, the bee just dances around in circles. But if they're more than 50 yards or so away, she performs a special waggle dance, running up and down the honeycomb, wagging her tail from side to side, then circling around and starting again. The angle of her run up the comb tells the other bees which direction to go in relation to the sun—running straight up says, "Fly directly toward the sun," while running straight down means, "Fly directly away from the sun." The number of tail waggings she does tells them how long they need to fly at a particular speed to reach the flowers. The fewer wags in a dance, the longer it will take to reach the flowers. If

there's a wind blowing in the wrong direction and it will take longer to reach a particular patch of flowers, she performs fewer wags than if there is no wind.

You can also train bees to fly to certain spots at certain times of day by putting out food in those places at those times. Like the migrating birds and the hibernating squirrels, they'll do this even if you keep them away from daylight. They've obviously got an internal clock that keeps track of the time of day.

Actually, bees aren't the only ones with a daily clock: we all seem to have one—animals, plants, bacteria, fungi, you name it. Plants can be surprisingly regular timekeepers—just as some plants flower only at certain times of year, so some flowers open regularly at particular times of day. The great botanist Carolus Linnaeus, who lived in Sweden in the eighteenth century, suggested making a floral clock by planting a bed with several different kinds of flowers and telling the time from which of them were open at that moment. He may never have grown a floral clock himself, but several people have done so since.

13

Carolus Linnaeus

As for us humans, all sorts of things that our bodies do change regularly over the course of a day. Some are obvious: we usually get tired in the evening and hungry about three times a day. Other changes we don't notice so much, but they're still important. Our body temperature, for example, is at its lowest at around four in the morning and at its highest in the early evening. This affects how well we do different things—for example, we seem to be better at exercising when our body temperature is at its highest, which may explain why athletes have often broken records when they run races in the evening.

These different daily rhythms are called circadian rhythms. (*Circadian* means "about a day" in Latin.) They're driven by a clock inside us—actually, not just one clock but millions and millions of them. It seems that all our cells contain molecular clocks run by different genes being switched off and on in a particular order. These molecular clocks are kept in time with one another by a master clock that sits in the middle of the brain. It's tiny (much smaller than the head of a pin) but it's very important—if it's damaged, our timekeeping goes haywire. This master clock works by sending out regular impulses that make sure all the organs in the body are coordinated. It also receives nerve signals from the eyes that tell it whether it's light or dark. These signals help it keep time with the real time of day, since, if left to its own devices, it would run slow by a few minutes each day. Such signals also allow our body clocks to adjust to changes in the length of day and night throughout the year and get over jet lag (eventually).

15

Chapter Three

So if we humans are equipped with a perfectly good biological clock, why did our ancestors become obsessed with calendars and mechanical clocks? We'll never know for sure, nor do we know when people first began to make calendars and count off days and months and years. But it must have been at about the time when humans first began to worry about the future and to think about how the world worked—why things happened when they did and what made them happen.

Early humans would have noticed that the world around them was always changing, often in regular ways, but sometimes in surprising ones. The most obvious regular change was from day to night and back again, and there was also the ebb and flow of the seasons. In tropical parts of the world, there were rainy seasons alternating with dry seasons, while away from the equator, winter would give way to spring, followed by summer, then fall, then winter again. Animals and plants changed with the seasons—some birds would appear in spring and disappear in autumn, while trees would always flower and fruit and shed their leaves at particular times.

Those early humans must have noticed regular changes in the heavens, too: the sun rose every day in the east and set every night in the west, and each night the great pattern of stars—the constellations—revolved in a circle around one point in the sky. The moon waxed and waned, and in summer the sun was above the horizon for much longer than in winter. The sun also rose and set in slightly different places each day and reached a different height in the sky—in winter it would stay low over the horizon, while in summer it would be overhead at midday. The constellations rose and set at slightly different times, too.

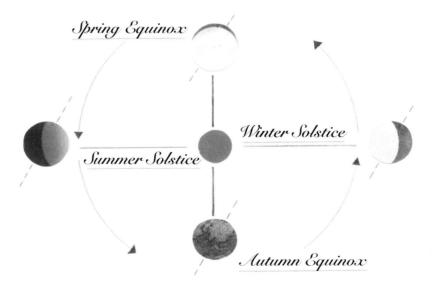

But lots of irregular and unpredictable things happened, too. Fierce storms might blow up, bringing deadly thunder and lightning; the rains could fail, causing drought; or huge swarms of locusts might appear out of nowhere, devouring everything in sight. Mountains—that is, volcanoes—could suddenly explode into fire or start belching out poisonous fumes. In the skies a few of the brightest objects (actually planets) moved *very* oddly, shooting stars could sometimes be seen, and even comets—strange lights that moved across the sky for nights on end—appeared from time to time. Very occasionally, part or even all of the sun or the moon went dark, even when there were no clouds.

Our early ancestors would have seen all this and tried to make sense of it. They thought that there were gods and spirits everywhere who made pretty much everything happen. They believed that the stars and the sun and the moon were either gods or places where gods lived. Some gods, like the sun god, were regular in their habits, while others, like the thunder god, were moody and unpredictable—but they evidently all had great power over human lives.

If you wanted to make sure that the right things happened in the future—that you would be victorious in battle or that the autumn storms would not destroy your home—then you'd want to keep the gods happy. That would mean holding ceremonies for them and making offerings and sacrifices, often in particular sacred places at particular times.

If you were a farmer, your life might depend on the coming harvest being good, so you'd do everything you could to make sure that it happened. If you relied on regular floodwaters to fertilize your land, for example, you'd want to hold ceremonies for the gods who controlled the rivers before the flooding was due to happen, to make sure they were in a good mood. To work out when the floods were due, you'd need some sort of calendar.

Also, once you'd decided that the sun, moon, and stars were important, you'd want to know what they were going to do in the future. Anyone who could know that would become a powerful person. Being able to predict dramatic events in the sky—like eclipses—would be incredibly impressive, a sure sign of having magical powers or being able to speak directly to the gods. Of course, if the rest of your tribe relied on you to know when things were going to happen, it could be rather risky if you got things wrong—*not* predicting an eclipse or a heavy flood might have bad, not to say fatal, consequences.

And that's probably why so much effort was put into developing calendars in so many parts of the world and why calendars and religion are almost always closely linked.

Chapter Four

Setting up a calendar wouldn't have been too difficult. All you would have to do is take something that seemed to happen regularly and count off the number of days before it happened again. The moon would be a good place to start, since it's very big and obvious in the sky and changes over a short period. Watching the moon and counting carefully, you'd quickly discover that a new moon appeared about every 29 days. You could then decide to hold a ceremony on the fourth new moon from now and be able to tell everyone how many days that would be. But you'd soon find out that a lunar calendar wouldn't keep very good track of the seasons or match the movements of the stars.

A calendar that followed the seasons needed to be measured over a longer time than a lunar calendar, and since the seasons were obviously connected to the sun, basing your calendar on the sun would be sensible. Using a gnomon—a stick in the ground that cast a shadow—you could mark the length of the shadow at the time of day when it was at its shortest, that is, when the sun was at its highest point in the sky. The length of the shadow would change from day to day, growing gradually longer and then shorter again. By careful counting and with a lot of patience, you would discover that the day when the shadow was at its shortest came around pretty much every 365 days. This was also the time when most of the stars would be back in their original positions in the sky.

So now you would have a moon calendar for marking short periods of time, as well as a sun calendar for marking longer periods. Surely all you had to do was combine the two and you'd have one calendar for all your needs, right? But the trouble was, the two just didn't fit together. Trying to combine them caused the ancients a lot of headaches, especially since they didn't understand what was causing all the changes, anyway. Nowadays we do understand—but it still hasn't helped us make a particularly logical calendar.

29 days

24 Hours.....

So why *is* it so difficult to set up a regular calendar? It has to do with the way the solar system works.

The Earth is a planet spinning at an almost unchanging speed on its own axis (which is like an imaginary stick going through the middle of the Earth from the North Pole to the South Pole). It takes almost exactly 24 hours for the Earth to spin around once and come back to where it started, and that, of course, is where our day comes from.

At the same time, the Earth is revolving around the sun in a path called an ellipse, which is like a slightly squashed circle. It takes almost exactly 365¼ days to make one complete circuit around the sun—which is what

365 Days and a bit

our year is based on. The axis that the Earth rotates around is tilted relative to the way the Earth revolves around the sun. That means that for half the year, the northern half of the world leans toward the sun and the southern half leans away. During that time, the days in the Northern Hemisphere are longer than the nights, while in the Southern Hemisphere, the opposite is true. For the other half of the year, the northern half of the world leans away from the sun, and the nights in the Northern Hemisphere are longer than the days. Twice a year, the days and nights in both hemispheres are exactly the same length. These are the equinoxes, and in our calendar they fall on or around March 21 and September 21.

old crescent

last quarter

waning gibbous

full moon

waxing gibbous

first quarter

new crescent

new moon

While the Earth is going around the sun, the moon is going around the Earth. It takes just over 29½ days to make one complete circuit, which is where we get our months from. Of course, while the moon is going around the Earth, the Earth itself is still spinning on its axis once every 24 hours, and that is why the moon seems to rise and set like the sun and the stars. The moon doesn't produce its own light—what we see is the reflection of sunlight bouncing off its rocky surface. The phases of the moon, that is, its regularly changing shape, have to do with the positions of the Earth, the moon, and the sun and the amount of the sun's light that is reflected back to us from the moon.

Light from sun

The stars that form the constellations are vast distances away and form an almost unchanging pattern in the sky, as though they were fixed in space. When we see them move through the sky, it's because of the spinning Earth, not because they are revolving around us.

The wandering lights in the sky are other planets like the Earth in our solar system. Five of them were known in the ancient world: Mercury, Venus, Mars, Jupiter, and Saturn. Each is revolving around the sun in its own path and at its own speed. Mercury whizzes around in just 88 of our days, while Saturn takes 29 Earth years. Because their orbits don't match ours, they're always changing their positions relative to the Earth. No wonder the ancient astronomers found them hard to keep track of.

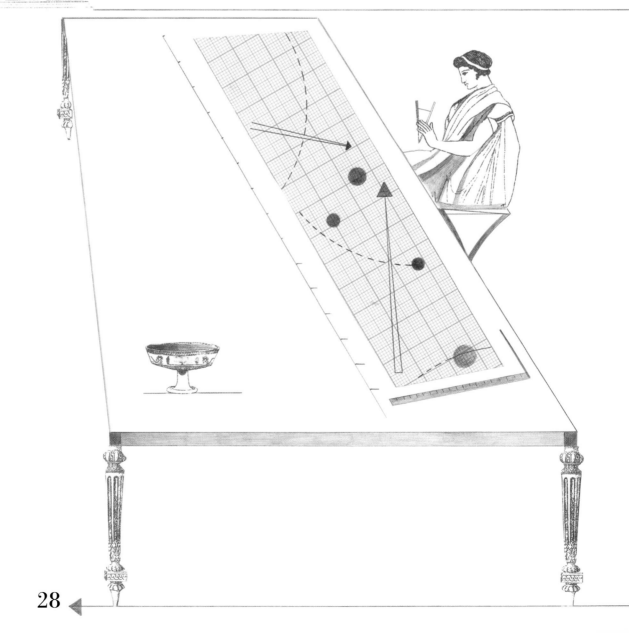

Chapter Five

Given all these complica-
tions, it's not surprising that
so many different calendars
have been developed. The
Mayans, who lived in Central America
and whose civilization was at its peak in
around AD 600–900, came up with one of the
most extraordinary calendars. They weren't very
interested in technology (they had the wheel once
and seem to have given up using it), but they were
obsessed with time, numbers, and astronomy. Their
months had just 20 days in them, and they had two kinds
of years, a sacred year of 13 months, or 260 days, and a year
based on the sun, with 365 days. To set dates, they combined
these to make a 52-year calendar, which they used to make incredibly accurate astronomical predictions about the movements of the
planets — more accurate than anybody else could manage at the time.
The Mayans later developed another calendar that had a unit
called a *baktun,* which was 144,000 days long. They believed that after
a great cycle of 13 *baktuns,* the world would be destroyed and recreated
again. Because their astronomical records were so precise, we can work
out that the most recent great cycle started on Wednesday, September 8, 3114
BCE. This means that it — and, according to the Mayans, the world — will come
to an end on Sunday, December 23, 2012. Don't say you haven't been warned!

Don't need that!

The
Mayans
didn't pay
much attention to
the moon in developing
their calendar. This saved
them a lot of trouble, as it's
proved impossible to come up with
a regular calendar that combines the
movements of the sun and the moon and
doesn't need to be adjusted on a regular basis. The
ancient Egyptians didn't even try. Instead they had two
separate calendars. One was a very practical calendar for
recording history (usually the great achievements of the Pharaohs)
and setting dates for the collection of taxes. It had 12 months of 30
days with an extra five days at the end, making 365 days in all. However, it
quickly got out of sync with the seasons, as it didn't take into account the extra
quarter day in the real year. The other calendar, based on the moon, ran alongside
it and was used to work out the dates of astronomical events and religious ceremonies.

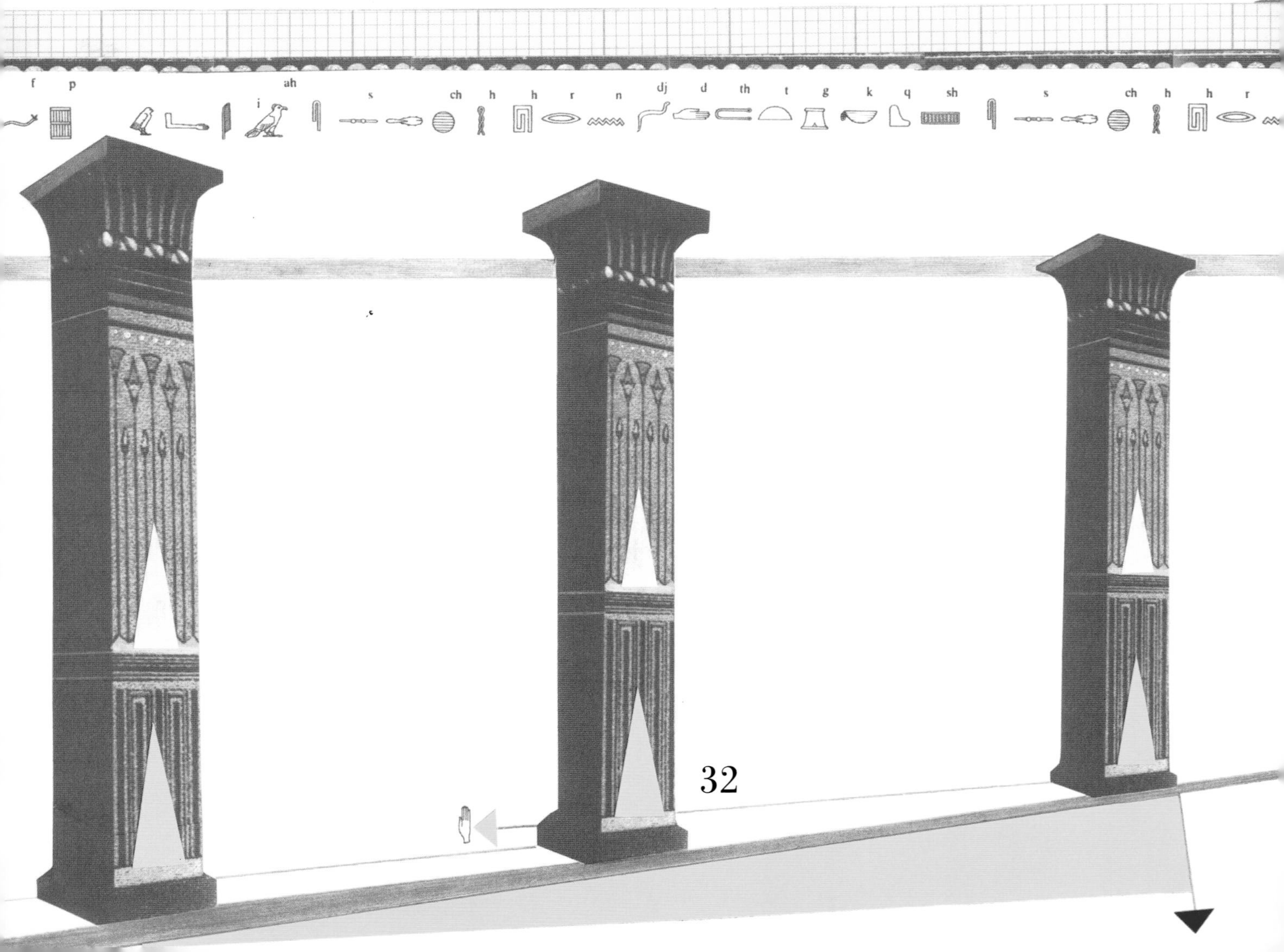

f p   ah dj d th t g k q sh   s   ch h h r n   m f p

1_2 x
30 + 5

= 365

The ancient Romans took the year to be 365¼ days but followed the moon in setting their months. They tried to keep things matched up by sticking in an extra short month every other year. If they'd done this sensibly, they wouldn't have had much trouble, but the people in charge—called pontiffs—didn't behave themselves. They put in months of whatever length suited them—if they wanted to grab a few extra days of power, they'd add a long month; if they wanted to speed up the time when a rival had to leave office, they'd put in a short one. When Julius Caesar came to power, in 51 BCE, the calendar was about three months out of time with the seasons and was generally a terrible mess. So he decided to sort the whole thing out with the help of a Greek astronomer named Sosigenes.

The calendar was reset. As a result, the year 46 BCE went on for

383 409 415 441
358 373 385 398 410 420 444
357 375 397 414 440 44 5
340 342 347 376 391 405 412 423 442
326 338 354 365 389 390 406 417 437 436
308 309 339 349 348 377 380 401 427 430
296 306 327 333 344 350 362 368 379 384 413 395 419 429 434
273 298 305 319 328 343 351 361 363 374 388 399 407 403 424 426 438
280 283 284 295 310 322 332 336 341 353 364 371 383 393 396 400 408 416 428 435
251 272 285 286 301 313 321 334 345 352 360 370 372 378 386 394 402 404 411
242 259 274 287 291 292 312 316 329 337 346 359 367 387
260 250 264 279 282 300 290 294 311 313 315 318 324 331 335 355 356 381 369
254 268 281 289 293 323 320 325
240 256 261 263 278 302 307 317
245 262 269 271 277 288 299
270

an amazing 445 days instead of 365—ever after known as the Year of Confusion!

The new calendar started in January 45 BCE, kept the normal year at 365 days, and introduced a leap year of 366 days every fourth year. Every other month (January, March, May, July, September, and November) had 31 days, and the remainder had 30, except February, which had 29 days in normal years and 30 days in leap years. With alternating long and short months, this scheme was neat and easy to remember—although Caesar didn't have much time to enjoy it himself, as he was assassinated the following year. But his efforts were commemorated by having the month Quintilius renamed in his honor as Julius (our July). Unfortunately, Caesar's calendar was messed up some years later, in 7 BCE, apparently because Emperor Augustus stole a day from February for the month he had named after himself (Augustus—our August). The lengths of September, October, November, and December all had to be switched around so as not to have three long months in a row. And that's why we have the odd system of days in the month that we use today.

Caesar's calendar—the Julian calendar, as it was known—was adopted by the Christian church and spread throughout Europe. However, it wasn't quite correct. Caesar hadn't taken into account the fact that the true length of the year wasn't exactly 365¼ days—it was 11 minutes (and 14 seconds) shorter than this. Very, very slowly, the Julian calendar slipped out of time with the seasons. Midsummer Day and the spring and autumn equinoxes moved forward in the calendar by about one day every 134 years. This was scarcely important during any one person's lifetime, but over the centuries, the effect built up.

Nobody would have worried had it not been for the problem of when to have Easter, which was worked out from the timing of the spring equinox. As the spring equinox got earlier and earlier in the calendar, Easter sometimes fell much sooner in the year than people thought it should. Eventually, it was decided that something had to be done, and in 1582 Pope Gregory launched a new calendar.

It established the system of leap years that we use now—leaving one out at the start of most centuries. But just as Caesar had had to have one long year to correct the calendar in his time, so Gregory had to introduce a short year to bring his calendar back in line with the seasons. The change wasn't as drastic this time around, but in the 1580s, it still meant losing ten days somewhere.

Today is the
1st of January.
Tomorrow
is the 12th.
OK?

Different places in Europe adopted the Gregorian calendar at different times. Italy, Portugal, Spain, France, and Poland took it on straightaway. Other countries, especially Protestant ones, were very suspicious of it, even though it made good astronomical sense. The Eastern Orthodox Church still hasn't accepted it.

Britain adopted the calendar in 1752. By this time, 11 days, not ten, had to be "lost," because the old Julian calendar that Britain was still using had fallen even further behind the seasons. The days chosen were the 3rd to the 13th of September, which simply vanished. It must have been very strange going to bed on the 2nd of September and waking up on the 14th! I'm sure you'd have been especially upset if your birthday had fallen in that period. Some people thought that 11 days of their life had been stolen from them, and there are even said to have been riots about it.

The Gregorian calendar is now the most widely used civil calendar in the world, but there are still plenty of others in use, particularly religious ones, such as the Islamic calendar, which strictly follows the moon, and the Jewish calendar, which uses complicated rules based on both the moon and the sun. And there have been lots of attempts to create a simpler calendar. In 1793 the French Revolutionary Parliament introduced one that, like the ancient Egyptian calendar, had 12 months of 30 days, with five days left over at the end of the year (six in leap years). The months were divided into three "weeks," each ten days long. The months were given names that described them: the fourth month (which started on December 21) was called *Nivôse,* meaning "snowy," while the fifth month, which started on January 20, was *Pluviôse,* or "rainy." This calendar didn't last very long, however, and on January 1, 1806, France went back to using the Gregorian calendar like most of the rest of Europe.

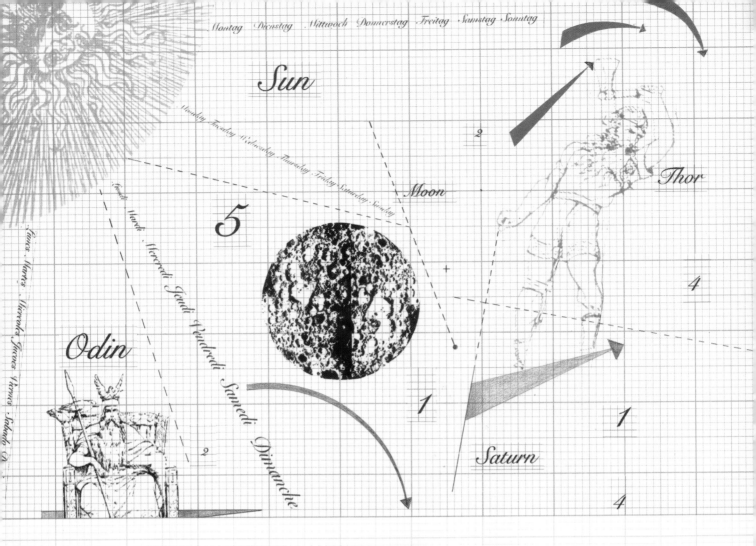

Chapter Six

The ancient Assyrians attached great superstitious importance to the days when the moon changed phase—the 7th, 14th, 21st, and 28th days after a new moon. These were unlucky days, and lots of activities, like preparing food or setting out on journeys, were forbidden. Instead, time was devoted to making sure that the gods were happy. This is where the idea of one day a week of rest and worship comes from.

Each day in the seven-day cycle was associated with one of the main celestial bodies (the five known planets, the moon, and the sun). The god or goddess linked to that body ruled over the day, and offerings would be made to him or her. These old gods live on in our modern names for the days of the week. In English, three of the names are directly linked

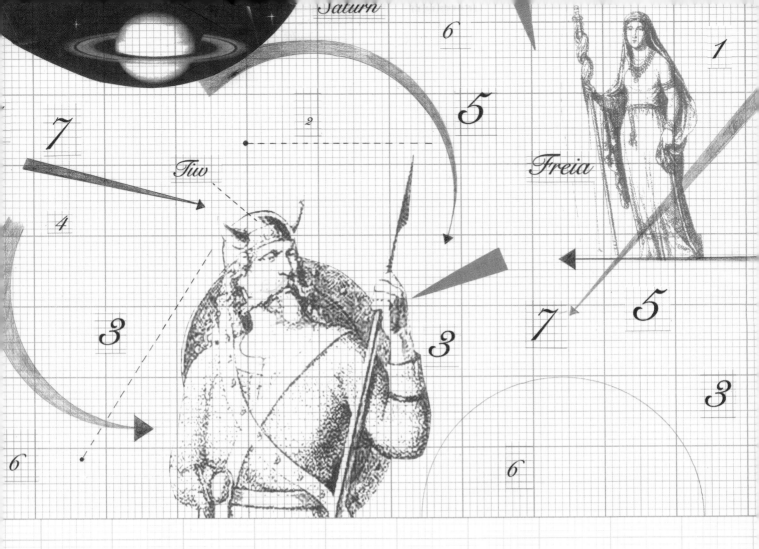

to the names of these celestial bodies: Saturn's day, the Sun's day, and the Moon's day. The other four days are named after Norse gods that were the equivalents of Roman planet gods. Tuesday is Tiw's day, named after the Norse version of Mars, the Roman god of war. Wednesday is Odin's or Wodin's day, for the Norse equivalent of the Roman god Mercury. Thursday is Thor's day, for the god of thunder, who was Jupiter, or Jove, to the Romans. Friday is Freia's day, for the goddess of the home, who was the Norse equivalent of Venus, the Roman goddess of love. Other European languages stick more closely to the Roman. In French, for example, Tuesday is *mardi* (Mars's day), Wednesday is *mercredi* (Mercury's day), Thursday is *jeudi* (Jove's day), and Friday is *vendredi* (Venus's day).

Chapter Seven

Calendars deal with long periods of time, sometimes incredibly long ones. The champion of these must be the Indian calendar, which has a period called the *Kali Yuga* that's 432,000 years long (the *Kali Yuga* started on Friday, February 18, 3102 BCE, so it's still got quite a time to run). At the other end of the scale are the little units we divide our days into—hours, minutes, and seconds.

As far as we can tell, the first people who measured short periods of time were the same people who developed calendars—astronomers or astronomer priests. Because they wanted to keep track of the movements of the stars, the moon, and the sun in detail, they needed to divide time into smaller divisions than just night and day. The ancient Egyptians were the first to divide the nighttime into 12 parts, based on the time at which different groups of stars called decans rose above the horizon. To match the 12 nighttime divisions, they also divided the time between sunrise and sunset into twelve periods. Altogether, that made 24 periods, which is where our 24-hour day comes from.

Unlike our hours, though, these Egyptian units weren't all the same length—during winter the nighttime hours were longer than the daytime ones, while in the summer the opposite was true. Only at the equinoxes, when night and day were the same length, were all the hours the same. Astronomers found these changing hours ever more of a nuisance as their scientific calculations became more advanced. Finally, in around 150 BCE, Greek astronomers decided to make all hours the same length, whatever the time of year. They took up the system used by the Babylonians, which divided things into units of 60, dividing their equal-length hours into 60 "first divisions," which we call minutes, and then into 60 "second divisions," which we call seconds.

The funny thing is, although they had come up with a division as small as a second, they couldn't even measure minutes accurately—it would take another 1,600 years and a lot of ingenuity for that to happen.

43

The earliest time-measuring systems that we know about were invented by the ancient Egyptians (them again) and were based on the sun during the day and the stars at night. The first sun clocks were simple T squares with lines marked on them that indicated the hours according to the length of the sun's shadow. Later, the Egyptians came up with primitive sundials, in which the time of day was shown by the direction of the sun's shadow rather than its length. At night they used instruments called *merkhets*. They could roughly tell the time by seeing where certain stars were between the two *merkhets*.

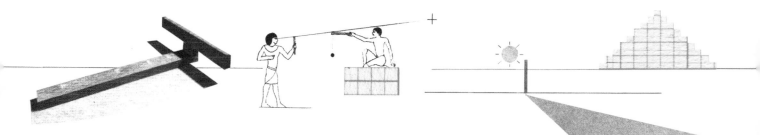

None of these methods was very accurate, however, and at some point (we don't know exactly when) the Egyptians—or it may have been the Babylonians—came up with a completely different way of measuring the time, using . . . water! By arranging for a steady flow of water into or out of a container with horizontal lines marked on the side—for example, using a cylindrical pot with a tiny hole in the bottom to maintain a constant drip—you can measure the time by where the water level is in relation to the lines. It seems simple, but it wasn't, because it's quite hard to keep water flowing steadily over a long period.

The ancient Greeks and Romans took up the idea of the water clock, which they called a *clepsydra*, and built some wonderfully elaborate and extravagant ones. Few people could afford their own, and those who could took great pride in showing them off and having a slave call out the hours. But *clepsydras* did have some practical purposes, too—like setting a limit to the length of speeches in the Roman Senate.

The most accurate water clocks in the ancient world were made not by the Europeans but by the Chinese. They had been using them since at least 600 BCE, but no one knows whether they got the idea from the Babylonians or the Egyptians, or whether they invented them separately.

The most amazing and elaborate Chinese water clock was created by a man named Su Sung in 1088. It lasted only a few years before it was dismantled, but luckily he had written a book in which he explained how the clock was made. In recent years several models of Su Sung's clock have been built, some of which can keep time to a minute a day, showing how accurate the original must have been.

In Europe during the Middle Ages, people also relied on water clocks, as well as sundials, to tell the time. None of these timepieces has survived, but we're sure that none was as accurate or magnificent as Su Sung's. A couple of hundred years after Su Sung, though, something amazing happened in Europe that would totally change the way we think about time—the invention of the mechanical clock. It's a mystery as to exactly where and when this happened, but it was probably sometime around 1280 and perhaps in England. We hardly know anything about the very first mechanical clocks, except that they must have been expensive, were usually installed in churches, and were almost certainly not at all accurate. The oldest one we know much about was designed by Richard of Wallingford for the Abbey of St. Albans in England in about 1328. It apparently didn't have a dial or hands but instead marked the hours with a hammer that hit a bell. It operated with an ingenious device called a verge-and-foliot escapement. This consisted of a bar (the foliot) that rotated backward and forward around a central rod (the verge) that controlled the way a toothed wheel turned. The wheel was driven by a weight suspended from a drum.

A craze for the new clocks swept through Europe. Clocks were designed and built that didn't just chime the hours but, like Su Sung's water clock, had moving models of the planets as well. The most famous of these was built by an Italian, Giovanni de' Dondi, in Padua between 1348 and 1364. But these clocks couldn't keep time precisely, constantly needed adjusting, and were hard to keep in good working order. Still, they had their uses (apart from being shown off), mostly to call people to prayer and tell them when to start and stop working in the towns and surrounding fields.

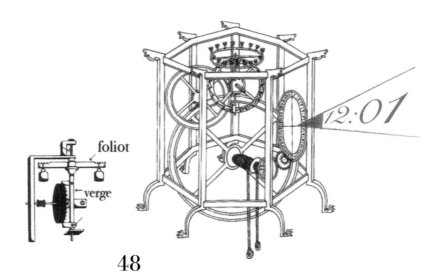

Giovanni de' Dondi

Chapter Eight

For the next couple of centuries, people depended on these not-very-accurate mechanical clocks and sundials to measure the passing of time. They also had the hourglass by now—it was invented at about the same time as the mechanical clock and was especially useful on ships, since, unlike mechanical clocks, it worked perfectly well when bobbing up and down.

During the fifteenth century, someone came up with the idea of driving clockwork with a spring instead of a weight, which meant that it was possible to build tiny clocks that could be carried around. Thus the pocket watch was born. These new watches were masterpieces of miniaturization—but they still weren't very accurate.

Then, in the seventeenth century, things suddenly changed. Scientists like the Italian Galileo Galilei and the Frenchman Marin Mersenne discovered that pendulums, which swing back and forth at a regular rate, made extremely good timekeepers. The first pendulum clock, built by the Dutch clockmaker Christiaan Huygens in 1656, could keep time to around ten seconds a day. By the end of the century, clocks that were accurate to half a second a day were quite common—though not *that* common, since they were very expensive and only the rich could afford them. At about the same time, the invention of a new kind of spring, the "balance spring," did for watches what pendulums had done for normal-size clocks.

Pendulum clocks became ever more precise in their timekeeping. A hundred years after Christiaan Huygens, the Englishman John Harrison made one that was accurate to a staggering one minute in ten years! Not only that, but it kept time perfectly at sea, a truly amazing achievement, which helped solve one of the most important problems of the age: how a ship could work out how far east or west it had traveled on its voyage.

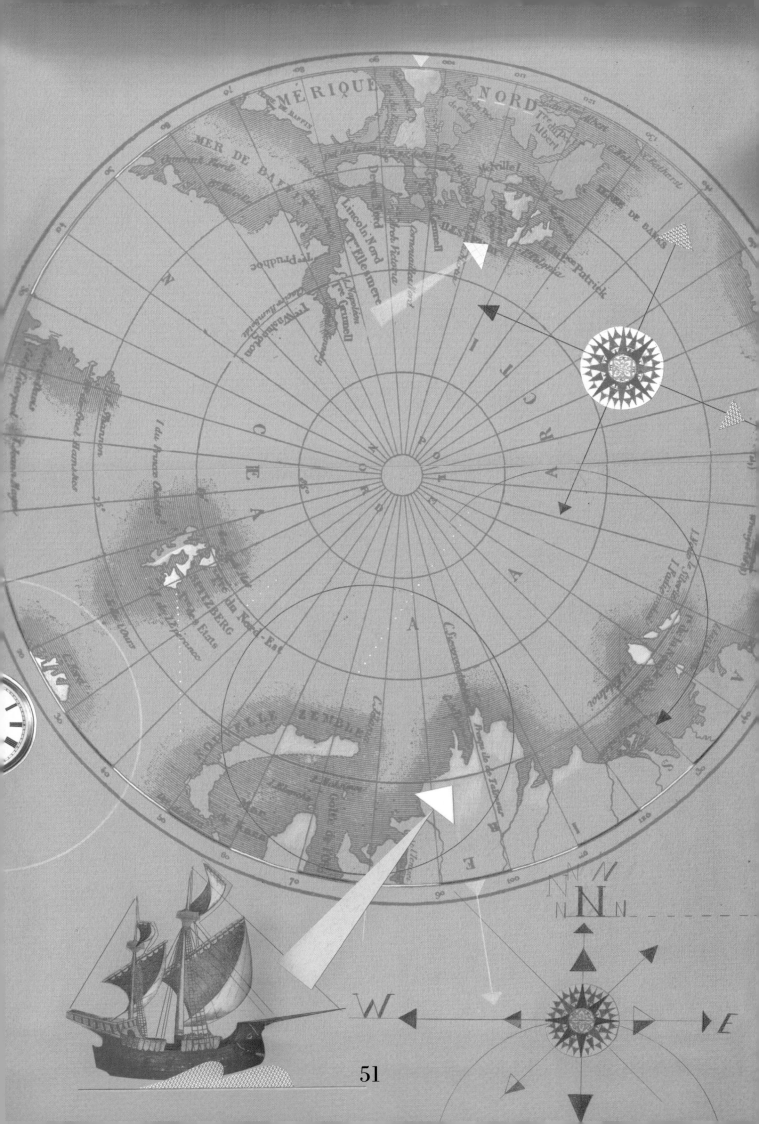

Chapter Nine

It wasn't until the twentieth century that timekeeping took another real leap forward. At the beginning of the century, it was discovered that quartz crystals vibrated at a regular rate if an electric current was passed through them. Because of these reliable vibrations, quartz could be used to keep time. The first quartz clocks were about the size of a wardrobe and weren't much better than the very best mechanical clocks—they kept time to around one second in five years. They soon improved, so that the best modern quartz clocks don't go off by more than a second in 275 years. Even that pales into insignificance compared with the next generation of clocks, which are based on the vibrations of individual atoms. The latest versions of these are accurate to within one second in 70 million years.

Timepieces haven't just become hugely more accurate; they've become much smaller and cheaper, too. You can buy a perfectly reliable quartz alarm clock or watch for the cost of a T-shirt or two. Not that you need to these days, as the time is everywhere—on mobile phones and computers, on the radio and on television, often fed directly to you from one of those atomic clocks that's correct to a billionth of a second. There's no excuse for being late for class or missing that train!

A hundred years ago it wasn't like this at all. Although clocks and watches were by no means rare, they were still expensive luxuries for working people, who mostly relied on the town-hall clock, the station clock, or the factory whistle to tell them the time. A hundred years before that, there wasn't even an agreed-on time to tell: each town and city stuck to its own time, which was generally the one on the clock of the most important church in town. Twelve noon by the clock in Boston might be 15 minutes later than 12 noon in New York. It didn't really matter—it would take several days to travel by the fastest stagecoach from one to the other, so a few minutes here or there made no difference, and no one got upset if you were ten minutes or half an hour late for a meeting.

1 o'clock

2 o'clock

3 o'clock

The railways changed all that. Trains ran on strict timetables; they wouldn't wait for anyone, and they could whisk you from one town to another at a speed undreamed of just a few years earlier. It became important that people were punctual and that everyone knew what the time was wherever they were. Britain, where the railways were first developed, became the first country to standardize its time. The time kept by the Royal Observatory in Greenwich, near London, was chosen as the standard, and by 1855 almost all the public clocks in the country were set to it. A timekeeping signal was transmitted across the country through electric cables laid along the railway tracks. Other countries gradually followed suit in setting their time.

Platform *1*

London
Waterloo

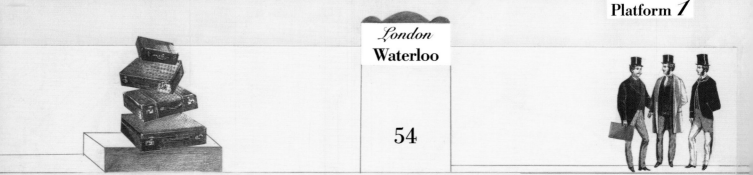

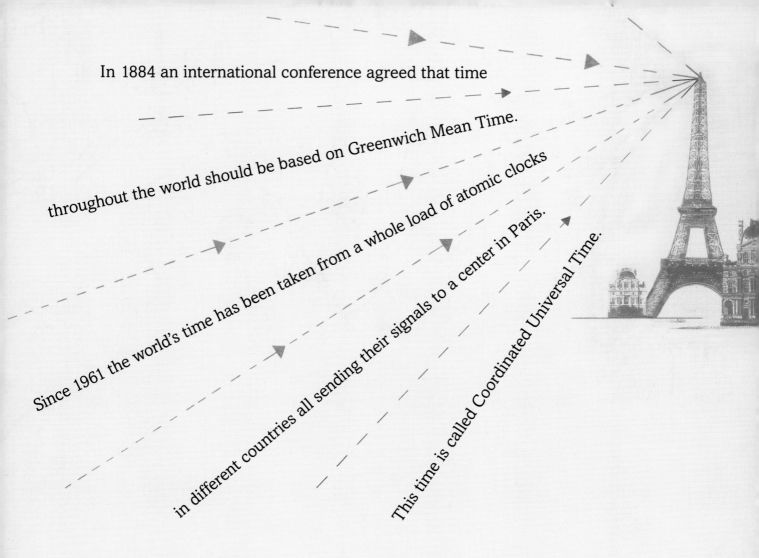

In 1884 an international conference agreed that time

throughout the world should be based on Greenwich Mean Time.

Since 1961 the world's time has been taken from a whole load of atomic clocks

in different countries all sending their signals to a center in Paris.

This time is called Coordinated Universal Time.

So here we are today with a time that all the world agrees on, accurate to a thousand-millionth of a second. And we know exactly how long it takes for the Earth to spin once around on its axis and for the Earth to go around the sun. We've even got a pretty good idea of how many years old the universe is (about 13.7 billion at the last count). It seems as if we've got it all figured out. But despite all this, do we really understand time at all?

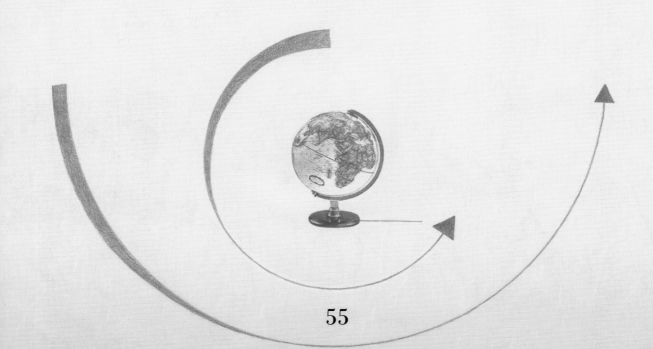

Chapter Ten

Well, it seems that the more we find out about time, the stranger it becomes. A hundred years ago, Albert Einstein showed that time didn't necessarily run at the same speed for everyone—it could stretch out or shrink depending on how fast you were moving. He called this his theory of relativity. You can only notice a difference in time speed when you're traveling very fast indeed—at nearly the speed of light (670 million miles per hour). We humans can't travel at anything like that speed, but we can see the effect of relativity by looking at the tracks left by minuscule subatomic particles called mu-mesons.

If we *could* travel incredibly fast in spaceships (and it's certainly not a complete impossibility), then some very strange things would happen. Imagine a pair of twins, one an adventurous astronaut and the other a homebody. The astronaut sets out in a spaceship traveling at about five-sixths the speed of light to visit the nearest star to Earth (other than the sun), which is around 4.2 light-years away (about 25,000,000,000,000 miles), then whizzes home again. According to the clock on the spaceship, the round trip takes about five years, which means the astronaut is five years older when she gets back to Earth. But back on Earth, almost *ten* years have gone by, so her twin is ten years older than when she waved the spaceship off—she's aged almost twice as fast as her space-traveling sister. It's weird, but it's true.

There are other ideas about time that we're less sure about. Some people believe it's made up of tiny particles, far, far smaller than an atom, that can't be divided into smaller pieces. Others think that time is part of the bits of string that they believe make up the universe. Then there's the possibility that one day the universe will stop expanding and start to shrink back in on itself, and time will run backward, so we'll all get younger and younger rather than older.

I don't know about any of that, but I still think time flies when you're having fun and drags when you're not. On that I'm sure we all agree.

Nearest star

25,000,000,000,000 miles

5/6 speed of light

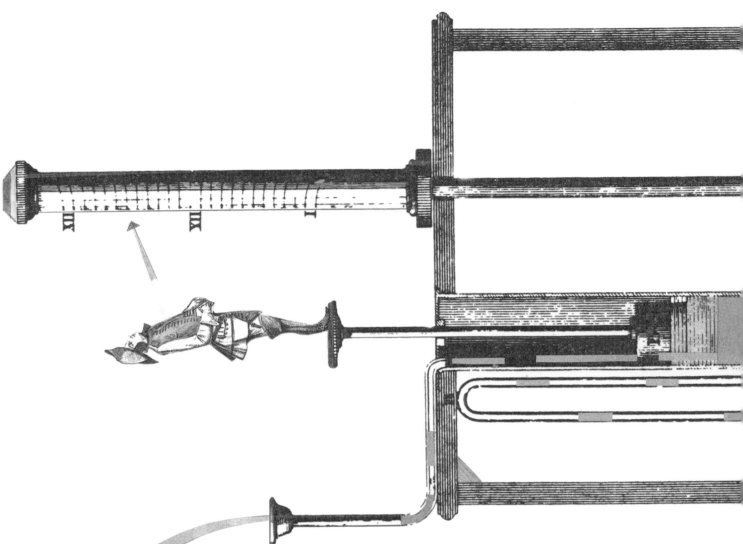

Index

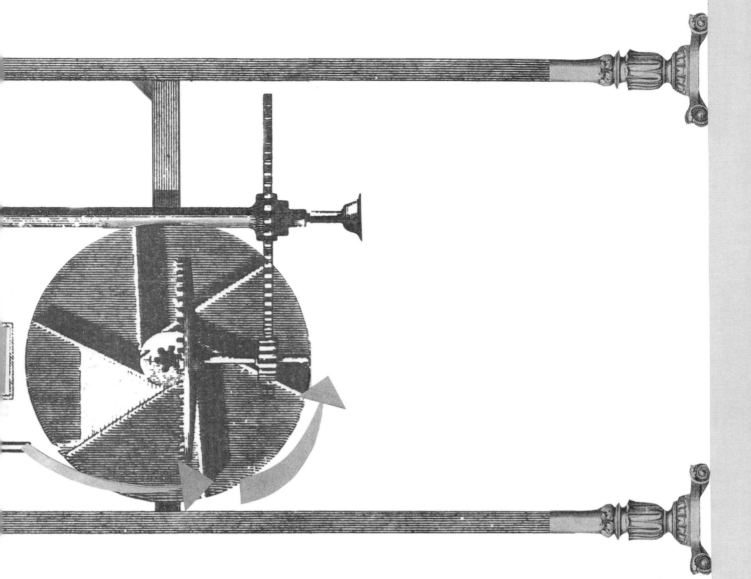